	MY	
MERCURY MERCURY MERCURY MERCURY		MERCURY MERCURY MERCURY MER
VENUS VENUS VENUS VENUS	**VERY**	VENUS VENUS VENUS VENUS VEN
EARTH EARTH EARTH EARTH	**EXCITING**	EARTH EARTH EARTH EARTH EA
MARS MARS MARS MARS MARS	**MAGIC**	MARS MARS MARS MARS MARS
CERES CERES CERES CERES	**CARPET**	CERES CERES CERES CERES CERE
JUPITER JUPITER JUPITER	**JUST**	JUPITER JUPITER JUPITER JUPIT
SATURN SATURN SATURN	**SAILED**	SATURN SATURN SATURN SATU
URANUS URANUS URANUS	**UNDER**	URANUS URANUS URANUS URANU
NEPTUNE NEPTUNE NEPTUNE	**NINE**	NEPTUNE NEPTUNE NEPTUNE NEP
PLUTO PLUTO PLUTO PLUTO	**PALACE**	PLUTO PLUTO PLUTO PLUTO PL
ERIS ERIS ERIS ERIS ERIS	**ELEPHANTS**	ERIS ERIS ERIS ERIS ERIS ERIS

A trick to remember the
names of the planets in order from the Sun
by National Geographic Planet Contest winner
Maryn Smith

11 PLANETS

A New View of the Solar System

DAVID A. AGUILAR

NATIONAL
GEOGRAPHIC
WASHINGTON, D.C.

**Published by the
National Geographic
Society**

John M. Fahey, Jr.,
*President and
Chief Executive Officer*

Gilbert M. Grosvenor,
Chairman of the Board

Tim T. Kelly,
*President,
Global Media Group*

Nina D. Hoffman,
*Executive Vice President;
President, Book Publishing
Group*

**Prepared by the
Book Division**

Nancy Laties Feresten,
*Vice President, Editor
in Chief, Children's Books*

Bea Jackson,
*Director of Design and
Illustrations, Children's Books*

Amy Shields,
*Executive Editor, Series,
Children's Books*

Jennifer Emmett,
*Executive Editor, Reference
and Solo, Children's Books*

Carl Mehler,
Director of Maps

Staff for This Book

Nancy Laties Feresten,
Editor

David M. Seager,
Art Director

Lori Epstein,
Illustrations Editor

Lewis Bassford,
Production Project Manager

Jean Cantu,
Illustrations Specialist

Jennifer A. Thornton,
Managing Editor

Gary Colbert,
Production Director

Susan Borke,
Legal and Business Affairs

**Manufacturing and
Quality Management**

Christopher A. Liedel,
Chief Financial Officer

Phillip L. Schlosser,
Vice President

Chris Brown,
Technical Director

Maryclare Tracy,
Manager

Nicole Elliott,
Manager

Founded in 1888, the
National Geographic
Society is one of the
largest nonprofit scientific
and educational organizations in
the world. It reaches more than 285
million people worldwide each
month through its official journal,
NATIONAL GEOGRAPHIC, and its
four other magazines; the National
Geographic Channel; television
documentaries; radio programs;
films; books; videos and DVDs;
maps; and interactive media.
National Geographic has funded
more than 8,000 scientific
research projects and supports
an education program combating
geographic illiteracy.

For more information, please call
1-800-NGS LINE
(647-5463) or write to the
following address:

National Geographic Society
1145 17th Street N.W.,
Washington, D.C. 20036-4688
U.S.A.

Visit us online at
www.nationalgeographic.com/books
Librarians visit us at
ngchildrensbooks.com

For information about special
discounts for bulk purchases,
please contact National
Geographic Books Special Sales:
ngspecsales@ngs.org

For rights or permissions
inquiries, please contact National
Geographic Books Subsidiary
Rights: ngbookrights@ngs.org

Library of Congress
Cataloging-in-Publication Data
available upon request.

Trade edition
ISBN: 978-1-4263-0236-7
Reinforced library edition
ISBN: 978-1-4263-0237-4

Printed in the U.S.A.

Our Sun is a medium-size star. Its gravity holds eleven planets and countless rocky asteroids and icy comets circling around it. The planets are divided into three groups based on size, how tightly packed they are (density), and what they are made of (composition).

In orbits closest to our Sun are the small, dense, rocky worlds of Mercury, Venus, Earth, and Mars. They are called the terrestrial planets—the Latin world *terra* means "land."

Ceres

Mars

Earth

Venus

Mercury

Jupiter

Sun

area filled with rocky leftovers from when the solar system formed. Hiding inside the asteroid belt is a new type of planet—a dwarf planet—named Ceres.

Located beyond the asteroid belt are the gas giants—Jupiter, Saturn, Uranus,

and Neptune. They are monster worlds made of frozen gases surrounded by rings and numerous moons. Beyond the gas giants is the Kuiper belt—an area filled with comets and other objects. The Kuiper belt also contains the other two dwarf planets, Pluto and Eris.

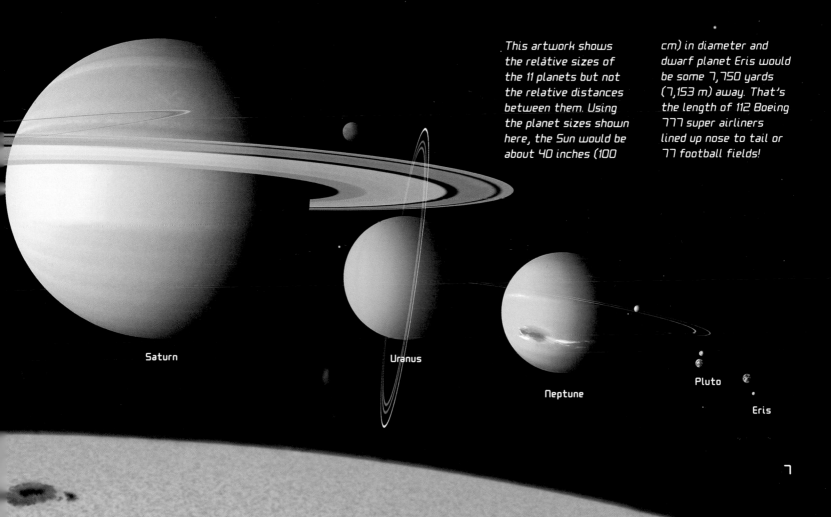

This artwork shows the relative sizes of the 11 planets but not the relative distances between them. Using the planet sizes shown here, the Sun would be about 40 inches (100 cm) in diameter and dwarf planet Eris would be some 7,750 yards (7,153 m) away. That's the length of 112 Boeing 777 super airliners lined up nose to tail or 77 football fields!

Saturn

Uranus

Neptune

Pluto

Eris

About five billion years ago, a huge star exploded into a supernova. It sent shock waves rippling through space, creating a swirling cloud of gas and stardust. As the cloud spun faster and faster, it formed a disk with a glowing red bulge at its center. That bulge slowly began to light up and eventually became our Sun.

At the same time, not far from the bulge, chunks of rock containing carbon, silicon, and ice lumped together to form small objects called planetessimals, which merged to become the terrestrial planets, which are also called the rocky planets. Located close to the intense heat of the Sun, these small worlds were rich in metals.

In the outer reaches of space, the planets took longer to grow as they gathered up lots of ice and methane gas to become gas giants.

Today we have a great mystery. Based on what we know about our solar system, astronomers know that smaller rocky planets like Earth form close to their stars. And they know that giant gas planets like Jupiter can only form much farther away. Yet scientists have now found nearly 300 planets around distant stars. Most of them are the size of Jupiter yet orbit closer to their suns than Mercury does to ours. How did these giants get there? Nobody knows.

Swirling
clouds of gas
and stardust

Dust disk
forming

Planetessimals
growing into
planets

Our solar
system today

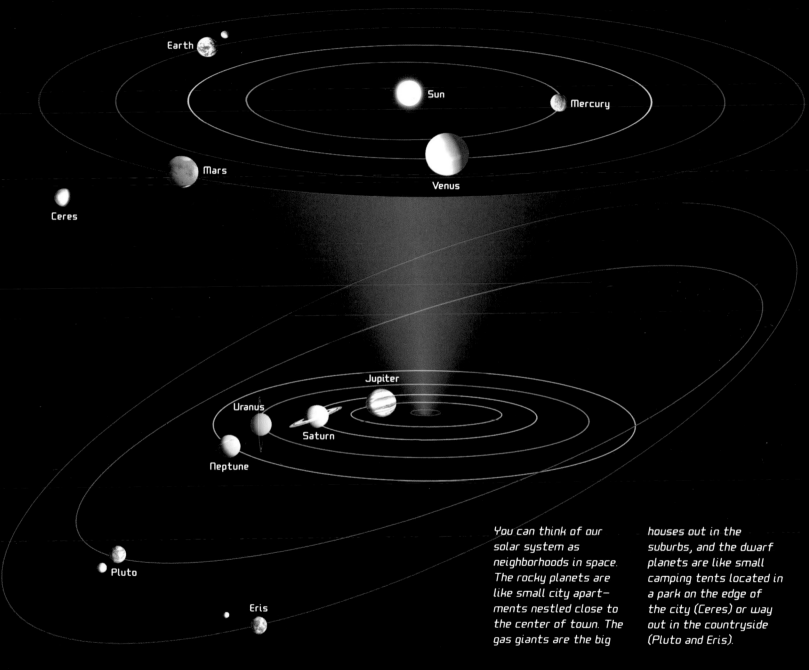

You can think of our solar system as neighborhoods in space. The rocky planets are like small city apartments nestled close to the center of town. The gas giants are the big houses out in the suburbs, and the dwarf planets are like small camping tents located in a park on the edge of the city (Ceres) or way out in the countryside (Pluto and Eris).

9

THE SUN

The Sun: Center of the solar system

Our Sun is the closest star to Earth. With its gravity, it anchors the solar system together. This yellow star is also the energy source that makes life possible here on Earth. The surface of the Sun averages about 10,000°F (5,000° C). It is a huge ball of burning gas composed of 74 percent hydrogen, 25 percent helium, and 1 percent trace elements, including iron, carbon, lead, and uranium. These heavier elements were created in the violent explosions of older stars.

Our Sun is a third-generation star. All of the heavier elements that are found inside the Sun, in Earth, and even in our own bodies were part of two other stars that came and went ages ago. Isn't it amazing to know that everything in our solar system is made from recycled stardust?

A giant solar flare erupts off the surface of the Sun. The flare will travel for millions of miles across space. Just one solar flare like this can unleash more energy than all the atomic bombs ever detonated. Imagine if we could harness all that free energy back here on Earth.

In ancient Greece and Rome, the Sun was the mightiest of all the gods. The Greeks named him Apollo. Apollo was life-giver to Earth and patron god of musicians and poets. Sunday is named in honor of the Sun.

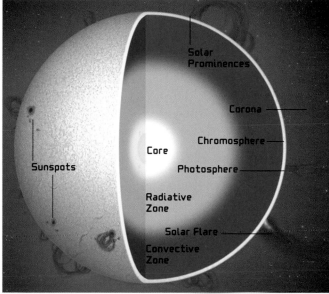

Solar Prominences
Corona
Chromosphere
Core
Photosphere
Sunspots
Radiative Zone
Solar Flare
Convective Zone

The bright surface of the Sun is called the photosphere. There sunspots, loops of gas called prominences, and explosive solar flares occur. The Sun's core is the nuclear furnace that sends heat out through the radiative zone, the convective zone, and the chromosphere until it reaches the surface. This process takes about one million years. Then, just nine minutes later, we feel the warmth here on Earth.

MERCURY

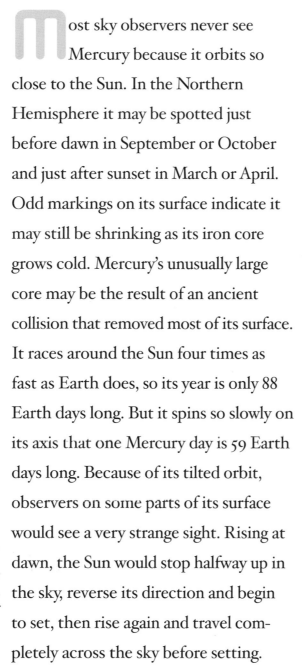

Most sky observers never see Mercury because it orbits so close to the Sun. In the Northern Hemisphere it may be spotted just before dawn in September or October and just after sunset in March or April. Odd markings on its surface indicate it may still be shrinking as its iron core grows cold. Mercury's unusually large core may be the result of an ancient collision that removed most of its surface. It races around the Sun four times as fast as Earth does, so its year is only 88 Earth days long. But it spins so slowly on its axis that one Mercury day is 59 Earth days long. Because of its tilted orbit, observers on some parts of its surface would see a very strange sight. Rising at dawn, the Sun would stop halfway up in the sky, reverse its direction and begin to set, then rise again and travel completely across the sky before setting.

Like our Moon, Mercury is pitted and scarred by craters, sharp cliffs, and ancient lava flows. Because it orbits between Earth and the Sun, it undergoes phase changes—from crescent to full and back again—when viewed from Earth.

With wings on his helmet and heels, Mercury was the speedy messenger of the gods. In the languages that come from Latin (including French, Italian, and Spanish), Wednesday is named after him.

Daytime on Mercury sizzles with temperatures reaching 800°F (427°C)—hot enough to melt lead and set your house on fire. On the night side, temperatures drop to a chilling -300°F (-183°C).

VENUS

Venus: Second planet from the Sun

Bright enough to be seen from Earth during the day, Venus has been called Earth's twin sister because they are about the same size. Blanketed in deadly clouds of carbon dioxide 40 miles (65 km) thick, Venus has the densest atmosphere of any planet in the solar system. A soda can dropped on the surface would be crushed by the atmospheric pressure. These thick clouds also work like windows in a car, trapping incoming sunlight. That trapped heat keeps the surface a blistering 864°F (462°C) day and night, making Venus even hotter than Mercury. The dim sunlight barely penetrating the clouds turns the barren landscape of this rock-covered world an eerie red. It is one of the driest places in the solar system, with no trace of water. Venus may be the closest planet to Earth and almost the same in size, but nothing else about it resembles our beautiful blue world.

The crescent Venus shines brilliantly, reflecting sunlight off the top of its solid cloud layer. Bright enough to cast a shadow on the ground at night, Venus is the third brightest object in our sky, after the Sun and Moon.

Venus was the Roman goddess of love, beauty, and springtime. The symbol for her bright shining planet is the hand mirror. Friday is her day of the week. The word for Friday in many languages means "Venus's day."

Like the Moon and Mercury, Venus goes through phase changes. When farthest from us, it appears small but is fully illuminated by the Sun. As it draws nearer, it grows larger in size but dimmer because part of it is in shadow.

EARTH

Earth: Third planet from the Sun

The third planet from the Sun shines like a blue gem with 71 percent of its surface covered by water. Its atmosphere is oxygen rich and filled with swirling white clouds. Spinning on its axis at 1,000 miles (1,600 km) per hour, it takes 365 days to make one complete trip around the Sun. Located at just the right distance from our star, Earth is not too hot or too cold. It is the only planet where water exists as a liquid, as a solid (ice), and as vapor in clouds. It also has the most diverse terrain of any planet. The outer crust, or solid rock surface, is just a thin layer covering a molten interior. In fact, if we reduced Earth to the size of an apple, the solid ground we walk on would be as thin as the apple skin. Yet, even on this fragile surface, life thrives everywhere—under the seas, in jungles, on mountains, in deserts, and even high up in the atmosphere.

No other planet resembles Earth. Blue and white from its oceans and clouds, our planet is teeming with life. In this artwork you can see both Earth and its companion Moon with the shadowed lines that divide night from day.

Gaea, the Earth goddess of the ancient Greeks, was known as the mother of Earth. Born out of chaos, she in turn gave birth to the sky, the seas, and the land. The Romans called her "Terra."

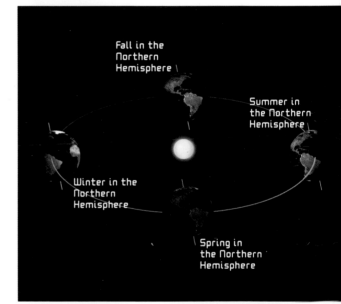

Fall in the Northern Hemisphere

Summer in the Northern Hemisphere

Winter in the Northern Hemisphere

Spring in the Northern Hemisphere

Seasonal changes are caused by the 23.5 degree tilt of Earth on its axis, not by how close it is to the Sun. When the Northern Hemisphere is tipped toward the Sun, it is summertime there and winter in the Southern Hemisphere. Six months later, when the Southern Hemisphere is tipped toward the Sun, it is summertime there and winter in the Northern Hemisphere.

EARTH'S MOON

About 4.5 billion years ago, while Earth was first forming, an object the size of Mars slammed into it and knocked big chunks off into space. The dust and rock from this crash formed a gigantic ring around Earth. Still hot and molten (melted), these pieces quickly came back together to form our Moon. Although Earth and the Moon are made out of the same material, they did not end up looking the same. On Earth, an atmosphere formed, oceans filled with water, and life began. On the Moon—too small to have the gravity necessary to hold onto an atmosphere—life never got started. So far, no water has ever been found on the Moon. The Moon's gravitation pulls on Earth's oceans, creating tides and in that way influencing life on Earth.

Standing on the Moon, we see just how different close neighbors can be. One is a vast wasteland and the other is an oasis for life. As campers have to bring their own food and shelter, astronauts have to bring all their own food, air, and water with them to the Moon. No living off the land here.

Near side with Mare

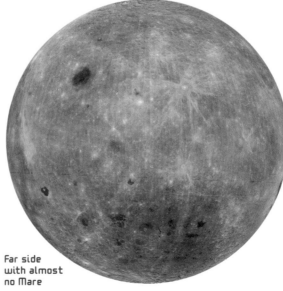

Far side with almost no Mare

The gravity between Earth and the Moon have slowed the rotation of the Moon so that one side always faces Earth. The side of the Moon that faces us (the near side) is quite different from the side that faces away (the far side). The dark flat plains we call Mare occur almost entirely on the near side. The Mare were caused by lava flowing out of ancient volcanoes and cooling. Scientists think the near side of the Moon had more volcanoes than the far side.

METEORITES

We see them streak across the night sky. We look up and say "Oh look—a shooting star!" Of course it isn't really a star. It's a piece of stuff from space burning up in our atmosphere. Drifting through space, these objects are called meteoroids. When they enter Earth's atmosphere, they are heated so hot they glow and are called meteors. If they hit the ground, they are called meteorites. Did you know Earth gains almost a ton of weight every day from meteorite dust drifting down from outer space? Most meteoroids are made of rock, but about eight percent are made of nickel and iron. Occasionally a really big meteorite strikes Earth, creating a gigantic crater.

Meteoroids need to be at least the size of a golf ball to make it to the ground. If they're smaller, they usually vaporize and sprinkle down from the sky as dust. There may be meteorite dust on top of your refrigerator right now.

Periodic meteor showers, ones that occur the same time every year, can be spectacular. They're the remains of comets that have passed by Earth, leaving small pieces of themselves behind.

MARS

Mars: Fourth planet from the Sun

Fifty million miles farther out into space, we find Mars—the last of the terrestrial planets. Like a piece of iron left out in the rain, the Martian soil has rusted red. Half the diameter of Earth, Mars has some spectacular scenery. The canyon Valles Marinaris dwarfs anything found on Earth. Seen in the artwork at left, it would stretch from New York to San Francisco. Mars has a volcano that stands 17 miles (27 km) high, large polar ice caps, and dust storms that can blanket the planet for months.

Someday humans may live on Mars, but it won't be easy. The carbon dioxide atmosphere is poisonous and so cold and thin that liquid water cannot exist on the surface. But the pink daytime skies, strange Martian sunsets, and limitless desert scenery may make Mars the perfect getaway spot for when you want to leave noisy neighbors on Earth behind.

This is how Mars might appear from its largest moon, Phobos. Off in the distance just to the right of Mars, smaller and more distant Deimos passes behind its planet. Both moons appear to be captured asteroids.

When Mars draws close to Earth, it appears blood red in color. This is why the Romans called Mars the god of war. His symbol is formed from a spear and shield. Tuesday is his day.

This spectacular image—taken by the HIRSE orbiter—is Victoria crater near the Martian equator. Almost half a mile (800 m) in diameter, this crater has recently been explored by the robotic rover Opportunity, which is now somewhere inside this 200-foot- (61-m-) deep hole in the ground.

CERES / ASTEROID BELT

Ceres: Fifth planet from the Sun

Astronomers were surprised when Ceres was discovered by accident in 1801. They immediately classified it as the fifth planet from the Sun, bumping Jupiter to sixth. In 1850 they changed their minds and reclassified it as an asteroid. In 2006, they decided it belongs in a new group of planets called the dwarf planets. Hidden deep inside the asteroid belt, Ceres takes 4.6 Earth years to orbit the Sun. About a quarter the diameter of our Moon, it is still the largest object in the asteroid belt.

Asteroids are leftovers from the early solar system and come in all shapes and sizes. Collisions between them happen a lot. Occasionally, Jupiter's gravity nudges an asteroid out of its orbit and sends it towards the Sun. Very rarely, one hits Earth. This can be disastrous. Just ask the unlucky dinosaurs!

Dwarf planet Ceres (top left in the artwork) is part of the asteroid belt between Mars and Jupiter. It is the biggest of thousands of objects left in this area from the formation of the solar system.

Ceres was the Roman goddess of fruit, vegetables, and agriculture. Her symbol is the curved scythe—the tool used to cut grains for the harvest.

The asteroids are rich in metals. Someday, space miners may dock with an asteroid like Eros (shown here) to harvest these pure metals and send them back to Earth. What might an asteroid be worth? A solid nickel–iron asteroid one mile (1.6 km) in diameter is worth an estimated 12 trillion dollars!

JUPITER

Jupiter: Sixth planet from the Sun

upiter is the biggest of the planets. All of the others could easily fit inside it. And with at least 63 moons circling around it, Jupiter is almost a miniature solar system by itself. The planet is made of hydrogen and helium gas with methane mixed in, so there is no solid surface to walk on. Its skies are blanketed with slushy frozen clouds filled with brilliant flashes of lightning and a giant red hurricane. Jupiter radiates heat—almost twice as much as it takes in from the Sun. It spins rapidly, making one rotation every 10 hours, and bulges in the middle. Jupiter would be a very smelly place to visit. The colorful brownish red stripes are made of ammonia hydrosulfide, which would smell like rotten eggs. The white clouds are made of ammonia, so they would smell like window cleaner. Jupiter also has rings, but they are too thin to see from Earth.

An ice sheet on Jupiter's moon Europa is a perfect viewing place. From here, we can see the Giant Red Spot—a hurricane that has raged for hundreds of years. Astronomers believe a vast ocean is hidden beneath Europa's ice.

Jupiter was the king of the ancient Roman gods, so his name works for the biggest planet. He was also called Jove, which is why the gas giants are sometimes called "Jovian planets." In some languages, Thursday is named for Jupiter.

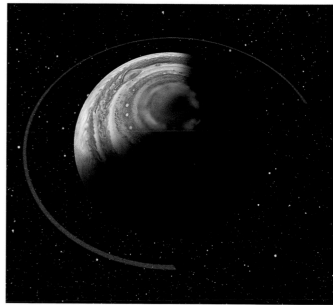

Jupiter generates one of the strongest magnetic fields in the solar system. This magnetic field bends energy particles from the Sun, resulting in beautiful green aurora that dance over Jupiter's north pole.

JUPITER'S MOONS

When Galileo first looked at Jupiter with his telescope, he couldn't believe his eyes. Four bright starlike objects formed a perfect line with the planet. Over the next few nights, these pinpoints of light moved along this line. Galileo realized at once—Jupiter had moons! This discovery helped convince Galileo that people of his time were wrong to believe Earth was the center of the universe.

Jupiter has at least 63 moons. The four largest can be seen through binoculars. Discovered by Galileo around 1610, they're called the Galilean moons.

Io is the closest to Jupiter. Though only the size of our own Moon, Io is home to over 150 volcanoes, which make it the most geologically active moon in the solar system. Europa is the second closest Galilean moon to Jupiter. Slightly smaller than Io, it has an icy surface that may cover a saltwater ocean. Third out is Ganymede—the largest moon in our solar system. The dark regions are old ice. The white spots are places where meteorite impacts have exposed newer ice. The fourth Galilean moon is battered and bruised Callisto. Scientists are not sure if a liquid ocean lies under its ice or if this moon is frozen solid.

1. The red, orange, and yellow on the surface of Io are sulfur and lava spewed out by active volcanoes. Because Io is located so close to warm Jupiter, it has no ice or water.

2. Underneath Europa's icy surface may be a warm saltwater ocean up to 60 miles (100 km) deep. Someday, underwater hydrobots may explore this ocean looking for signs of life.

3. Ganymede is larger than the planets Mercury, Ceres, Pluto, and Eris. Its icy surface is covered with meteorite craters and dust, but underneath the surface may be a liquid ocean like Europa's.

4. Callisto is the most heavily cratered object in the solar system. Its surface was formed some four billion years ago. Unlike the other three Galilean moons, it doesn't seem to have a molten core.

1. Io

2. Europa

3. Ganymede

4. Callisto

SATURN

Saturn: Seventh planet from the Sun

aturn is the most distant planet visible to the naked eye. Like Jupiter, it has no surface to walk on. Its frozen slushy atmosphere, made mostly of hydrogen and helium gas, forms faint bands across its surface. Saturn's density is so low that if you dropped it into water, it would float like a cork. Consisting of thousands of individual little bands called ringlets, Saturn has the most dazzling set of rings surrounding any planet. Composed of particles ranging from dust grains to giant boulders, they are the remains of a small moon or asteroid that was torn apart hundreds of millions of years ago. The rings are brighter than Saturn itself. Astronomers divide them into seven different bands labeled A to G. If you ever have the chance to look at Saturn through a telescope, do it! No other planet in our solar system is quite as beautiful.

This view from Saturn's moon Mimas shows how thin Saturn's rings are. If their diameter were reduced to the size of a football field, they would only be as thick as a piece of paper.

Because Saturn moves so slowly across the sky at night, the Romans associated it with the grandfather of the gods, Jupiter's father. The symbol for Saturn is the sickle—a tool used for cutting grain. Saturday is named for this planet.

Part of a storm hanging over Saturn's north pole, this hexagon-shaped cloud is 15,000 miles (24,000 km) across. It has persisted for almost 26 years. This picture was taken by the Cassini spacecraft.

SATURN'S MOONS

Saturn has at least 60 moons in all sizes and shapes. The largest and most mysterious is Titan. Hidden from view behind thick, rusty clouds, Titan may hold the key to the origin of life on Earth. Larger than the planet Mercury or any of the dwarf planets, Titan has a thick atmosphere, liquid lakes bigger than Lake Superior or the Caspian Sea, cryovolcanoes spewing out ice, wind-blown sand dunes, drizzling rain, and seasonal changes. The surface of Titan is primarily water ice and rock. The dense atmosphere is mostly nitrogen with orange-red ethane and methane clouds. This atmosphere closely matches the primitive atmosphere of Earth when life began 350 million years ago. Could there be extraterrestrial life on this distant cold moon? We may know within the next 20 years.

Smothered by layers of red and orange clouds, the landscape of Titan includes hydrocarbon lakes and rivers. It rains day in and day out on Titan, but instead of water, liquid methane drizzles down onto the surface, keeping it always wet and muddy.

Titan

Titan is the only moon in the solar system with a thick, hazy atmosphere. Its frozen surface is spotted with dark lakes of liquid methane.

Enceladus

Coated with fine crystals of ice from erupting water volcanoes, Enceladus reflects almost 100% of the sunlight reaching it back into space.

Iapetus

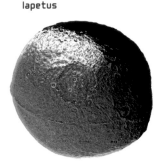

With one hemisphere colored black and the other colored white, Iapetus is the only two-toned moon in the solar system.

Mimas

Rocked by a collision that almost destroyed it, Mimas's most distinctive feature is the impact crater Herschel, which is almost 80 miles (130 km) across.

URANUS

Uranus: Eighth planet from the Sun

Because Uranus is tipped on its side, its rings face directly toward us. Recently, astronomers have detected that Uranus's inner ring is growing brighter, but they don't know why.

Uranus glows like an aquamarine gem because of the methane gas in its atmosphere. Resembling a tiny green pea when viewed in an amateur telescope, it is an icy giant about eight times the size of Earth. Unlike any other planet in our solar system, Uranus has a 98-degree tilt to its axis. Scientists think that early in its history it was hit by something really big that knocked it completely over on its side. Its rings turned sideways, too. Viewed straight on, it looks like a bull's-eye in space.

Right now, Uranus's north pole faces the Sun while its south pole faces away into space. This means the north pole is in its 42 years of sunlight, which will be followed by 42 years of darkness. There is no solid surface on Uranus. It is made mostly of hydrogen and helium gas like our Sun. Uranus has 27 moons, the third most behind Jupiter and Saturn.

Uranus was named for the Greek god who was the father of Saturn and the grandfather of Jupiter. The symbol is the sign for the metal platinum. Uranus was discovered in 1781. Until then, people knew about only six planets.

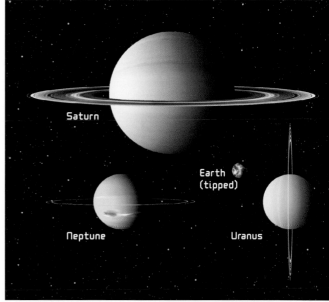

Saturn

Earth (tipped)

Neptune

Uranus

If Earth tipped on its side like Uranus, sunlight hitting the north pole would cause violent weather while the south pole would experience frigid darkness. Most life would be concentrated in a belt stretching around the equator.

35

NEPTUNE

Neptune: Ninth planet from the Sun

Neptune is the smallest gas giant and the farthest from the Sun. It also has the wildest weather of any planet in the solar system, with winds that blow at speeds of more than 1,200 miles (2,000 km) per hour.

Neptune has no solid surface to walk on. The temperature at the top of the cloud layer is a chilling -353° F (-214° C). However, its core remains hotter than the Sun's surface. This internal heat causes the violent winds and hurricanes.

Neptune was discovered using mathematical calculations. When scientists realized something big was affecting the orbit of Uranus, they calculated where that object might be in space. When they looked, there was Neptune! It is billions of miles farther out than Uranus. Since its discovery more than 160 years ago, Neptune still hasn't completed one full orbit around the Sun.

The blue methane clouds of Neptune reflect light onto the frozen surface of its moon Triton. Some astronomers believe Triton formed farther out in space, migrated in, then was captured by Neptune's gravity.

Neptune is the Roman god of the sea. This is fitting for a planet colored like the oceans. His symbol is the trident—an ancient fishing spear.

Like the other gas giants, Neptune has hurricane-type storms. Almost the size of Earth, the Great Dark Spot on Neptune was first imaged in 1982 by the Voyager spacecraft. It has disappeared since this picture was taken.

PLUTO

Pluto: Tenth planet from the Sun

10

For the last ten years of his life, Percival Lowell, the astronomer famous for believing he had discovered canals on Mars, searched for a "Planet X" beyond the orbit of Neptune. As hard as he tried, he never found it. In 1930, 14 years after Lowell's death, Clyde Tombaugh—a 22-year-old night assistant at the observatory named after Lowell— discovered Pluto. For 76 years Pluto was the ninth planet from the Sun. Then, in 2006, it was demoted to a dwarf planet and, with the addition of Ceres, became the tenth planet from the Sun. Because Pluto's moon Charon is so large, some astronomers consider Pluto and Charon a double-planet system. Located at the fringes of the Kuiper belt, Pluto travels in an egg-shaped orbit around the Sun, sometimes crossing inside the orbit of Neptune to temporarily become the ninth planet again.

Pluto was the Roman god of wealth and the underworld. The planet's symbol is the combination of the letters P and L. They stand for astronomer Percival Lowell, who searched for Pluto.

Stars in the Milky Way help illuminate Pluto, its two smaller moons Nix and Hydra, and erupting ice volcanoes on its large moon Charon as they cross the orbit of Neptune. In the distance, dust from the asteroid belt creates a fuzzy glow around the Sun.

Pluto is one of the coldest objects in the solar system. When it reaches its farthest distance from the Sun, its atmosphere freezes and falls to the ground, where it looks like a thin coating of sugar frosting.

Eris: Eleventh planet from the sun

Eris is the coldest and most distant planet in our solar system, with an orbit that is more oval than round. Larger than Pluto and made of rock and ice, this dwarf planet travels with its moon Dysnomia through an area called the Kuiper (rhymes with "wiper") belt and ten billion miles past it.

The Kuiper belt is an area of our solar system that extends from the orbit of Neptune billions of miles into space, where it may merge with the Oort cloud. There are five Kuiper belt objects that may someday be added to the list of dwarf planets. The oddest one is named EL61. (I call it "Eggland" because it is shaped like a chicken's egg.) In the future, scientists may decide to split the dwarf planets into two categories—asteroid belt dwarfs like Ceres and Kuiper belt dwarfs like Pluto and Eris.

The dwarf planet Eris and its moon Dysnomia orbit the farthest reaches of our solar system. Eris's discovery in 2005 led to the debate that resulted in the new category of dwarf planet.

Eris was the Greek goddess of discord, or fighting. She was always causing trouble. According to legend, when she offered a golden apple to the prettiest goddess, the resulting arguments caused the ten-year Trojan Wars.

About 16 miles (26 km) long by 10 miles (16 km) wide, egg-shaped EL61 almost blocks out the distant sun. It is surrounded by debris left behind when our solar system formed 4.6 billion years ago.

41

Comets are objects orbiting our Sun that can suddenly appear in our sky. Made of sand, water ice, and carbon dioxide, comets have been best described as dirty snowballs. Some—including Halley's Comet—come from the Kuiper belt, but most come from the Oort (rhymes with "port") cloud and can take millions of years to complete one trip around the Sun. As comets move in toward the Sun, they begin to defrost. As they draw nearer to the Sun, solar energy vaporizes their ices, forming a round halo, or coma. Soon, a long, spectacular tail blown by the solar winds may emerge, stretching for millions of miles across space. Some 800 comets have visited the inner solar system in recorded history. Scientists think there are trillions more out in the Oort cloud.

Astronomers believe the Oort cloud is the remains of the solar nebula that collapsed to form our solar system. This cloud may extend halfway to the Sun's nearest star neighbor, Proxima Centauri, which is shown on the lower right with an Oort cloud of its own. It would take 100,000 years for a space shuttle to fly from the Sun to Proxima Centauri.

The spectacular tail of a bright comet stretching for millions of miles through space lights up the sunset skies over Earth. The word "comet" comes from the Greek word "kometes," which means "hairy star."

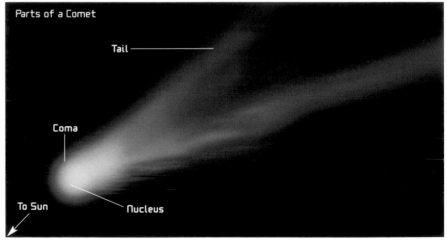

Parts of a Comet

Tail

Coma

To Sun

Nucleus

Comets are composed of a tiny nucleus of rock and ice that becomes surrounded by a gaseous coma as it heats up. As a comet draws closer to our Sun, long separate tails of gas and dust can form—they always point away from the Sun.

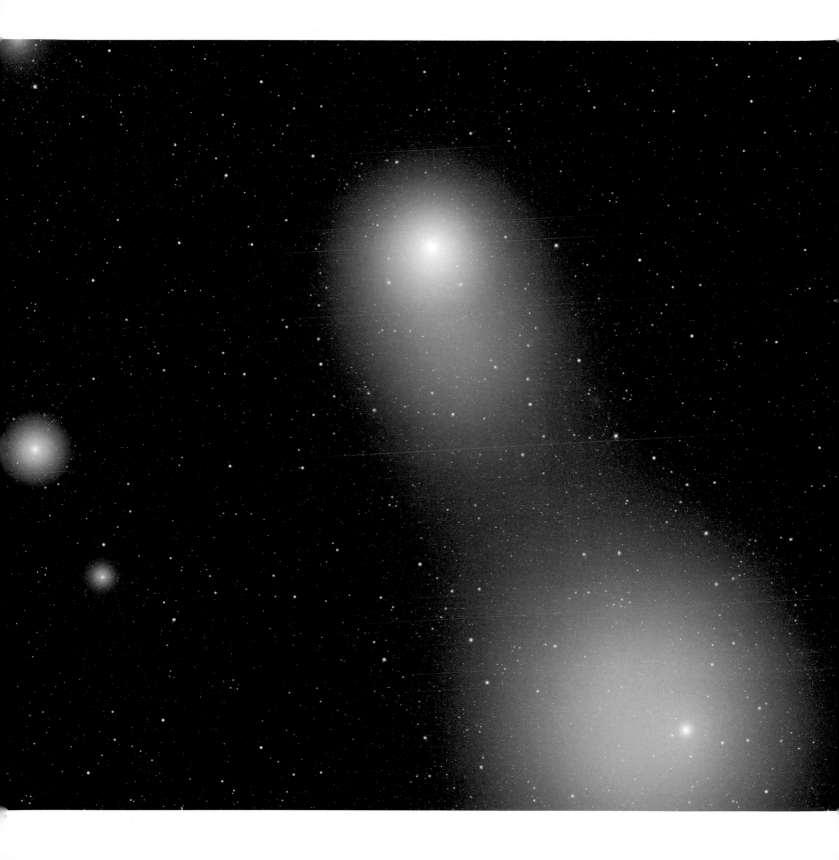

This is an exciting time for astronomy. Almost every week another planet is discovered orbiting a distant star. These new worlds fall into two categories. The first group is called "hot Jupiters" because they orbit extremely close to their stars, are larger than Jupiter, and are made out of gas. The second group is called "super Earths." They are made out of rock and ice and are two to three times the size of Earth. These planets orbit cooler red stars about half the size of the Sun. Is there any life on them? It seems unlikely. They are too close to their stars and too hot. However, super Earths with orbits farther out would be perfect for alien life.

Orbiting a red dwarf star 9,000 light-years away, this super Earth is about twice the size of our planet. Its year (one orbit of its star) takes only 10 Earth days.

About 60 light-years from Earth in the constellation Vulpecula, this hot Jupiter named HD 189733b orbits its star at a distance of only 3 million miles (5 million km). Earth orbits 93 million miles (150 million km) from the Sun.

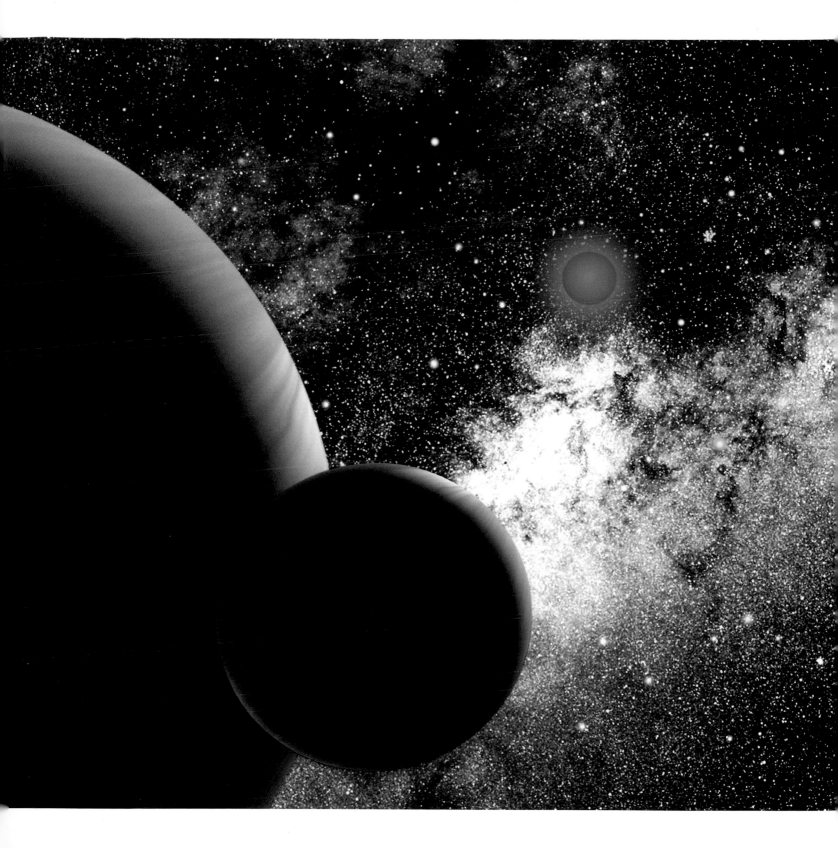

Cryovolcanoes
Volcanoes that erupt frozen gases such as ammonia, methane, and water. They are found on the moons of gas giants and on dwarf planets.

Dwarf planet
One of a new class of small planets that includes Ceres, Pluto and Eris.

Extraterrestrial life
Life originating outside Earth. Most scientists believe it exists, but none has yet been found.

Extrasolar planet
A planet that orbits a star other than our Sun.

Gas giant planet
One of a class of large planets composed mostly of frozen hydrogen, helium, and ices. The gas giant planets in our solar system are Jupiter, Saturn, Uranus, and Neptune. There is no surface or ground on a gas giant, so they would be impossible to walk on.

Hot Jupiter
A Jupiter-size extrasolar planet that orbits very close to its star, which makes it very hot. Hot Jupiters are the easiest extrasolar planets to detect from Earth.

Light-year
The distance light travels in a vacuum in one year. It equals 5,878,625,373,184 miles (9,460,730,472,581 km). It is used as a measurement for distance in space.

Meteor
A meteoroid that travels through the Earth's atmosphere, leaving a streak of light as it burns up.

Meteorite
A meteor that hits the ground.

Meteoroid
Small particles of metal or stone that travel through space. Most come from asteroids broken apart by collisions with other asteroids.

Methane
A colorless, odorless gas. It is the principal component of natural gas used for cooking and heating homes.

Moon
A round body that orbits a planet.

Molten
Melted by extreme heat. Many planets and moons have molten rock at their center.

Nebula
A gas cloud that is the remains of an exploded star.

Orbit
The path of a celestial body or an artificial satellite as it revolves around another body.

Photosphere
The visible bright outer layer of the Sun.

Planet
A large, round body that orbits a star.

Red dwarf star
A cool, very faint star about half the size of our Sun. Red dwarfs are the most common type of star in the universe.

Solar flare
A sudden violent explosion of energy that occurs in the Sun's atmosphere near a sunspot.

Solar nebula
A cloud of dust and gas from which stars and planets form.

Solar prominence
An arc of gas between two sunspots. Prominences can loop hundreds of thousands of miles into space from the Sun's surface.

Sun
The star that is the center of our solar system.

Sunspot
A dark marking on the Sun's surface caused by a magnetic storm. It appears dark because it is slightly cooler than the surrounding area.

Super Earth
A rocky extrasolar planet two to four times larger than the Earth.

Supernova
A giant star that has grown old, run out of fuel to burn, and exploded, sending star materials out into space.

Terrestrial planet
One of a class of planets primarily composed of silicate rocks. Also known as a rocky planet. The terrestrial planets in our solar system are Mercury, Venus, Earth, and Mars.

Compare your Earth weight with how much you'd weigh on other planets									
Earth	Moon	Mercury	Venus	Mars	Ceres	Europa	Titan	Pluto	Eris
50/23	8/3.5	19/9	45/20	19/9	1.5/0.7	6.7/3	7.5/3.4	3/1.4	3.1/1.4
60/27	10/4.5	23/10	54/24	23/10	1.8/0.8	8/3.5	9/4.1	4/1.8	4.1/1.9
70/32	11.5/5.2	26/12	63/29	26/12	2.1/1	9/4.1	11/5	4.6/2.1	4.7/2.1
80/36	13/5.9	30/14	72/33	30/14	2.4/1.1	10.5/4.8	12/5.4	5.3/2.4	5.4/2.4
90/41	15/6.8	34/15	82/37	34/15	2.7/1.2	12/5.4	14/6.4	6/2.7	6.1/2.8
100/45	17/7.7	38/17	91/41	38/17	3/1.4	13.4/6.1	16/7.3	6.7/3	6.8/3.1

Jupiter, Saturn, Uranus, and Neptune are not included because they have no surface, so it would be impossible to stand on a scale to weigh yourself. The figures above are in pounds/kilograms.

Name	Mercury	Venus	Earth	Mars	Ceres
Meaning	Roman messenger of the gods	Roman goddess of love	Unknown	Roman god of war	Roman goddess of agriculture and of motherly love
Sun Position	1st	2nd	3rd	4th	5th
Class of Planet	Rocky	Rocky	Rocky	Rocky	Dwarf
Diameter	3,030 miles (4,878 km)	7,520 miles (12,100 km)	7,900 miles (12,750 km)	4,222 miles (6,794 km)	585 miles (940 km)
Density	5.43 g/cm³	5.25 g/cm³	5.52 g/cm³	3.94 g/cm³	2.08 g/cm³
Shape of Orbit	⬭	○	○	○	○
Temperature	-300°F (-183°C) to 800°F (427°C)	864°F (462°C)	-126°F (-88°C) to 136°F (58°C)	-270°F (-133°C) to 80°F (27°C)	-159°F (-106°C)
Number of Moons	none	none	1	2	none
Rings	no	no	no	no	no

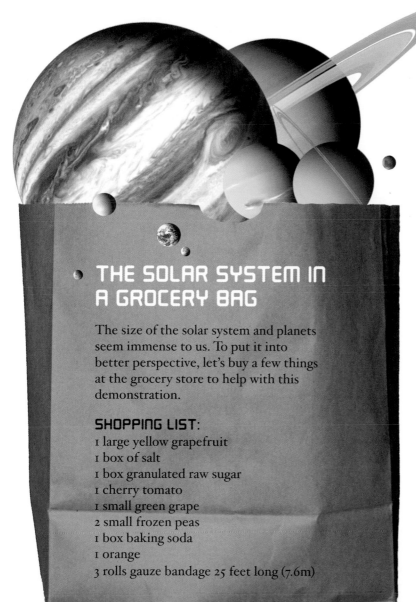

THE SOLAR SYSTEM IN A GROCERY BAG

The size of the solar system and planets seem immense to us. To put it into better perspective, let's buy a few things at the grocery store to help with this demonstration.

SHOPPING LIST:

1 large yellow grapefruit
1 box of salt
1 box granulated raw sugar
1 cherry tomato
1 small green grape
2 small frozen peas
1 box baking soda
1 orange
3 rolls gauze bandage 25 feet long (7.6m)

If we use a grapefruit to represent our **Sun**, the planet **Mercury** will be the size of a small grain of salt, 18 feet (5.5 m) away from the grapefruit.

Venus will be larger than Mercury, about the size of a grain of raw sugar, located 34 feet (10.4 m) away.

Earth, also the size of a grain of raw brown sugar, will be 50 (15 m) feet away.

Mars, the size of a grain of salt, is 75 feet (23 m) away.

Ceres, a speck of dust, is located 150 feet (46 m) away.

Jupiter, a cherry tomato, is 240 feet (73 m) away.

Saturn, our green grape, is 420 feet (128 m) away.

Uranus, a frozen green pea, is 300 yards (274 m), or 3 football fields, away.

Neptune, another green pea, is 470 yards (430 m) away.

For **Pluto,** pick up a speck of baking soda and place it between 465 and 600 yards (425 and 549 m) away. (Pluto's orbit is not nice and round like the other planets, so its distance from the Sun varies.)

Eris, another speck of baking soda, should be between 900 and 1050 yards (823 and 960 m) away.

For a **Comet,** tie three rolls of gauze bandage together end-to-end to make one piece about 70 feet (22 m) long. This is the size of the Great Comet of 1843.

And what do we do with that orange? It represents **Proxima Centauri,** the nearest star to our own Sun. Proxima Centauri is located 4.2 light-years away. To place it in proportion to our solar system, it would be about 2,400 miles (3,862 km) away from the grapefruit.

There you have it. This is our solar system (plus its neighboring star) to scale.

	Jupiter	Saturn	Uranus	Neptune	Pluto	Eris
	Roman king of gods	Roman god of agriculture	Greek god of the sky	Roman god of the sea	Roman god of the underworld	Greek goddess of discord or confusion
	6th	7th	8th	9th	10th	11th
	Gas Giant	Gas Giant	Gas Giant	Gas Giant	Dwarf	Dwarf
	88,846 miles (142,984 km)	74,898 miles (120,536 km)	31,500 miles (50,724 km)	30,775 miles (49,528km)	1,430 miles (2,302 km)	1,678 miles (2,700km)
	1.30 g/cm³	0.70 g/cm³	1.24 g/cm³	1.76 g/cm³	2.03 g/cm³	2.1 g/cm³
	○	○	○	○	⬭	⬭
	-235°F (-150°C)	-288°F (-178°C)	-323°F (-200°C)	-353°F (-214°C)	-369°F (-223°C)	-406°F (-243°C)
	at least 63	at least 60	27	13	3	1
	yes	yes	yes	yes	no	no

ACKNOWLEDGMENTS

Working at the Harvard-Smithsonian Center for Astrophysics in Cambridge, MA, I had some of the foremost experts in astronomy to call upon when I was writing this book. I would like to thank Dr. Owen Gingerich—Harvard research professor, astronomy historian, and chairman of the International Astronomical Unions' Planetary Definition Committee, Dr. Brian Marsden—Director emeritus of the Minor Planet Center at Harvard, Dr. Daniel Green—comet expert, Dr. Lisa Kaltenneger—extrasolar planet atmospheric expert and Smithsonian Young Astrophysicist of the Year 2007, Dr. Dimitar Sasselov—Harvard Professor and Director of the Harvard Origins of Life Initiative, Dr. David Charbonneau—extrasolar planetary discoverer and Scientist of the Year for *Discover Magazine,* Dr. Rick Fienberg—Editor in Chief of *Sky & Telescope* magazine, and J. Kelly Beatty—Executive Editor of *Sky & Telescope* magazine. And though of course he was not available to answer my questions, I want to thank Carl Sagan (1934–1996), whose legacy lives on in every new discovery made in astronomy.

FURTHER EXPLORATION

Here are some great Web sites that you can visit to learn more about the new solar system.

Calculate your weight and age in the solar system
http://www.exploratorium.edu/ronh/weight/
Fun Solar System Activities
http://science.hq.nasa.gov/kids/solar_system.html
http://www.kidsastronomy.com/fun/make-a-solar-system.htm
http://spaceplace.nasa.gov/en/kids/sse_flipflop.shtml
Hubble Site
http://hubblesite.org/
Author's Site
www.aspenskies.com
Astronomy Magazine Site
http://www.astronomy.com/asy/default.aspx
Sky & Telescope Magazine Site
http://www.skyandtelescope.com/
Astronomy Picture of the Day
http://apod.nasa.gov/apod/
Space.com
http://www.space.com/news/
Harvard-Smithsonian Center for Astrophysics
http://cfa-www.harvard.edu/

Contents

Preface

This is the third edition of *Game, Set, Match . . . A Beginning Tennis Guide* designed for the beginning tennis player. It is written for the student who is actively receiving tennis instruction, and who plans on continuing to play tennis as a lifelong physical activity.

There are several new features to this third edition that hopefully will enhance the learning experience of the beginning player. All chapters have been reviewed and adjusted where it seemed to make sense. The photographs and diagrams within each of these chapters have been updated, and they are now all in color, which provides a new perception and sense of the action and mechanics of tennis. All chapters have been revised and chapters on *Physical Aspects of Playing Tennis* (Chapter 6), *Mental Aspects of Tennis Competition* (Chapter 7), *Tennis Court and the Equipment Design* (Chapter 12), and *Tournament Competition and Resources in Tennis* (Chapter 13) have been revised extensively. In addition, the *USTA Tennis Rules* have been added in the appendix, a *Game, Set, Match Instructor's Guide* has been developed to assist the instructor in coordinating the use of the book with the practical experience of learning to play the game on the tennis court, and a new capsule learning aid, called *Cues*, has been added to the skill chapters. And finally, to add to the "new look" the material is presented in an 8 1/2 x 11 size to provide for easier reading and use of the book.

The chapters are developed in a logical sequence of learning experiences that include: basic tennis strokes; understanding of the behavior and rules that govern play; understanding of the game strategies; individual practice drills; coordination of mind and body into the mental aspects of play; and learning about court surfaces and equipment. Each chapter will assist the reader in understanding the game of tennis in a simplistic and clear manner. Photographs and diagrams provide visual samples of strokes, strategy, and basic concepts. Sections related to skill acquisition are reinforced with capsule learning experience suggestions, and with an "elimination of errors" review to facilitate an indepth understanding of those skills.

Tennis is a highly popular sport played at all levels of skill and by all ages. It requires a strong foundation of skill, and indepth comprehension of the intricacy of the flow of the game, and an insight into the rules of play. It is a game that is played at an intense level of competition by some and in a spirit of enjoyment by all who understand that tennis is a game. Tennis, as played today, is a never-ending learning experience for the player. It is a complex game that, when played and practiced over the years, becomes surprisingly simplistic and yet always remains challenging.

Game, Set, Match provides the beginning player with a visual and written analysis of tennis. Students will profit in their skill development by reading the descriptions of the skills and reviewing the photographs in order to gain a mental image of the execution of the skill. They also will gain from reading and understanding how physical fitness and mental preparation are critical to their improvement and development as a player. The two strategies chapters will provide a base for development of thinking on the court, and the etiquette and rules section will enable the student to make sense of the intangibles of tennis. There are also two informational chapters regarding the tennis court and equipment, and tournament play and resources that will aid the student in gaining a full understanding of the fringe parts of the game.

This material is truly a guide for the beginning tennis player who is taking instruction through courses or lessons and who will continue to grow with the game through the years.

James E. Bryant

ACKNOWLEDGMENTS

Since 1986 numerous individuals have contributed to the continual development of *Game, Set, Match* as reviewers, models, illustrator, and as sources to provide as accurate and complete of a book as possible. I want to extend a personal thank you to all of those who have in some way permitted me to gain from their knowledge and talents in order to write a book for the beginning tennis player that truly allows for skill development and growth. In particular, I want to convey a special thank you to my former students who have given feedback and served as a true test of the practicality and applicability for the book as designed for a beginning player.

Specifically, I want to thank those who have been instrumental in assisting in the development of this third edition. These people include photographer Eric Risberg who created the quality photographs that show tennis skill at its best, Richard Gonzales of the Cupertino Tennis Center, Cupertino, CA, who provided beautiful facilities for all of the photographs, Bob Schram who designed the great cover, and models Anh-Dao Ngyuen and John Hubbell, San Jose State University tennis coaches, who not only performed the proper skills to be photographed, but who also made appropriate suggestions that make the book that much better.

James E. Bryant

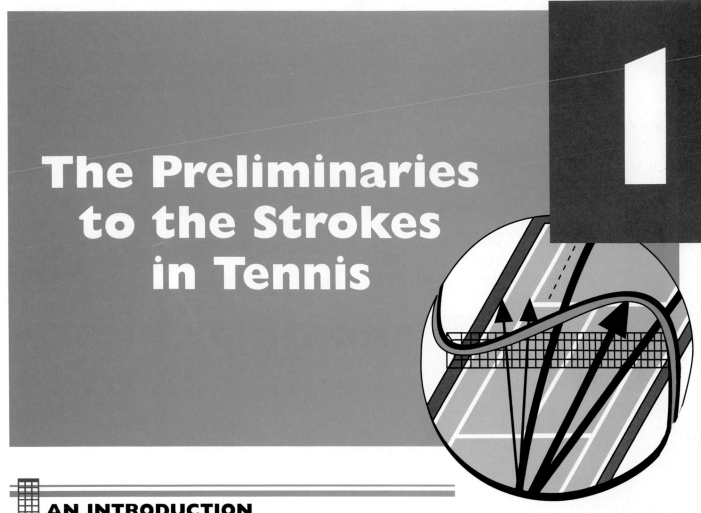

The Preliminaries to the Strokes in Tennis

AN INTRODUCTION

To play tennis, it is imperative to know how to hold a tennis racket for a particular stroke, and how to stand and move. Recognizing the spin of the ball, although not of immediate concern to the beginner, is extremely important as the player's skills develop. It is also wise to gain a comprehension of racket face control and have a feel for the ball as the racket impacts the ball. Learning how to grip and control a tennis racket, and how to get ready to hit the ball, are skills that must be established early in the learning experience.

BASIC TENNIS GRIPS

The use of a tennis grip when hitting a particular stroke is directly related to the execution of that stroke. The selection of a tennis grip that fits the stroke is necessary to complete the stroke with acceptable form.

The *eastern forehand grip*, a universally used grip designed for executing the forehand groundstroke, is also called the "shake hands" grip (Figures 1.1–1.3). Place your racket hand on the strings of the racket, and bring your hands straight down to the grip. As your hand grasps the racket grip, your fingers will be spread along the length of the racket grip with the index finger spread the furthest in a "trigger finger" style, providing control.

Figure 1.1 "Trigger-finger" position.

Figure 1.2   Eastern forehand grip (back view).

Figure 1.3   Eastern forehand grip (top view).

The thumb will be situated on the back side of the racket, and a "V" will be formed by the thumb and the four fingers on the racket grip. The "V" points to the racket shoulder when the racket is held in front of the player at a right angle to the body.

Figure 1.4   Eastern backhand grip (front view).

Figure 1.5   Eastern backhand grip (top view).

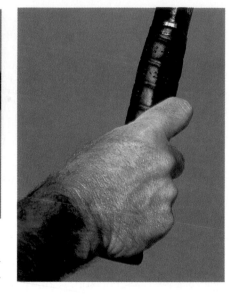

The *eastern backhand grip* is a conventional backhand grip used extensively in tennis (Figures 1.4–1.5). From the eastern forehand grip, roll your hand over the top of the racket grip and place your thumb diagonally across the rear plane of the racket grip. You should be able to see all four knuckles of the racket hand from this position when the racket is held perpendicular to the body. The "V" formed by the thumb and fingers will point to the non-racket shoulder when the racket is held in front of the body.

Figure 1.6   Forehand-backhand continental grip (back view).

Figure 1.7   Forehand-backhand continental grip (top view).

The *continental forehand grip* and *continental backhand grip* are essentially the same (Figures 1.6–1.7). They differ from the eastern forehand and backhand grips in that the hand is placed midway between the positioning of the two eastern grips. The "V" formed by the thumb and fingers points to the middle or center of the body halfway between the racket and non-racket sides of the body when the racket is held in front of the body. The subtle difference between the forehand

and backhand placement of the hands for the continental grip is that, in the forehand grip, the thumb grasps the racket grip, whereas in the backhand, the thumb is placed diagonally across the rear of the racket grip.

The *western forehand grip* (Figures 1.8–1.9) is often used by those who have received no instruction in tennis, or it is used for special strokes such as a topspin forehand groundstroke. The grip is best achieved by laying the racket on the court and picking it up naturally. The palm of the hand faces flat against and under the back side of the racket grip. The "V" formed by the thumb and fingers, when the racket is held in front of the body, points beyond the racket shoulder.

The use of the two-hand grips in tennis have become popular in recent years. The *two-hand backhand grip* (Figures 1.10–1.11) is achieved when the hand on the racket side grasps the racket grip in either a continental or eastern backhand grip, with the non-racket-side hand butted above that grasp in an eastern forehand grip. The two-hand backhand grip must be a snug fit of two hands working together to execute the stroke. There is also a two-hand forehand grip that is used by a few players, but the grip is not widely used at this time.

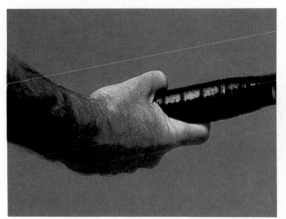

Figure 1.8 Western forehand grip (back view).

Figure 1.9 Western forehand grip (top view).

Figure 1.10 Two-hand backhand grip (front view).

Figure 1.11 Two-hand backhand grip (top view).

The selection of the grip is based on a particular purpose. Eastern forehand grips are used for the forehand groundstroke, while the eastern backhand grip is used for the backhand groundstroke and for special serves. The continental grips are used for groundstrokes, net play, and for serving. The continental grip has the added advantage of requiring little in the way of grip adjustment for different strokes; consequently, strokes are disguised when this grip is used. The western forehand is used with success when hitting topspin forehand groundstrokes. The two-hand backhand is a useful grip, particularly with individuals who lack the strength to hit with more conventional grips or who are seeking more power and control for their groundstrokes. The disadvantage to the grip is that the player lacks reach for wide shots. The two-hand stroke is excellent for players who are willing to move and react to every ball hit to them.

From the perspective of *what grip to use for what stroke situation*, it is suggested that the eastern grips be used by a player who intends to stay at the

Remember: All grips require that the index finger serve as a trigger finger to provide control of the racket along with a relaxed and flexible grip.

baseline and hit groundstrokes. When serving, use the continental grip — it will provide control, accuracy, and power for an effective service. As a beginner, you may want to start by using the eastern forehand grip for the serve; however, you should switch to the continental as soon as possible. Going to the net to play a volley shot requires reaction and timing, which means that the grip should not be changed much for a forehand or backhand volley. It is recommended that the player maintain a continental grip for play at the net to avoid miss-hitting the ball and being confused at the net.

LEARNING EXPERIENCE SUGGESTIONS
Grip

1. Keep the fingers spread down the racket grip with the index finger serving as a "trigger finger."

2. Be aware of the location of the "V" in relation to the racket and non-racket shoulders.

3. Grasp the racket firmly when assuming a grip.

4. Understand the subtle differences with each grip and the purpose for each grip.

ELIMINATION OF ERRORS (Grip)

The Error	What Causes the Error	Correction of the Error
Lack of control of the racket.	Grasping the racket in a vise-like position.	Make sure that the fingers are spread along the racket grip with a trigger finger.
Miss-hitting a ball or poor execution.	The grip is too tight.	Relax the grip. Grasp the racket firmly, not tightly.
	The grip is too loose.	Tighten the grip. Grasp the racket firmly, not tightly. Check grip size. The racket will turn in the hand when a return shot has high velocity if the grip is too small.
	Wrong grip for the stroke.	Check purpose for each grip.

CONTROLLING THE RACKET AND GETTING READY TO HIT

Racket control is essential to good strokes and thus to successful play. Three basic actions are taken when swinging a racket that will provide racket head control and that will consequently accomplish a stroke. The basic *swing action* is reflected in the forehand and backhand groundstrokes and the various lobs. The serve and overhead smashes are described through the *action of throwing*, while the *punch action* is used with forehand and backhand volleys. By executing each of these actions or patterns, you will eliminate all extraneous motion, which will help you to simplify the action of each stroke.

There are also three basic *racket face* positions that affect the control and flight pattern of the ball, followed by the bounce of the ball on the surface of the court. The effect of these three racket face positions on the resultant action of the ball is dependent on the speed of the racket head hitting through the ball and on the angle of the racket face when it contacts the ball. If contact is made with the *racket face flat* to the ball (Figure 1.12), the flight of the ball will be straight, with the ball falling to the court surface due to gravity. An *open racket face* (Figure 1.13) will cause the ball to have a floating action in its flight, spinning in a backward motion. A *closed racket face* (Figure 1.14) will force the flight pattern of the ball downward due to the ball having a forward spin. Each racket face position is important to all skill levels of players, and understanding what causes the drop or rise of the ball gives the beginning player a greater insight into the total concept of hitting the ball and reacting to the bounce.

Figure 1.12 Flat racket face.

Figure 1.13 Open racket face.

Figure 1.14 Closed racket face.

Comprehending spins is a direct carryover from understanding racket head and racket face control. A tennis shot that is hit without spin is affected by three aspects of the overall stroke. First, as the ball strikes the racket face, a direct force is applied to the ball that provides velocity and determines the flight pattern of the ball. Secondly, that velocity is countered by air resistance and gravity, with the former impeding the velocity of the tennis ball and the latter pulling the ball down toward the court. Finally, the ball will strike the tennis court surface at an angle equal to the rebound of the ball off the court surface.

When a ball spins in its flight pattern, the tennis player must also cope with the behavior of the ball as it strikes the court surface. There are three *basic actions for balls in flight* (see Figure 1.15). First, *topspin* is caused by the action of the top surface of the ball rotating against air resistance. This creates friction on the top part of the ball, forcing the ball in a downward path. A second spinning rotation, *underspin,* is caused by the bottom of the ball meeting air resistance and forcing the ball to stay up longer than is normally found with a non-spinning ball. The final spin action of a ball — *sidespin* — is created when the side of the ball meets air resistance and pressure. This causes the ball to veer to the opposite side.

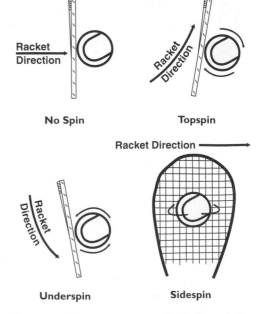

Figure 1.15 Basic actions for balls in flight.

The *action of the ball striking the court surface* is the end result of racket control action on the ball and the spin of the flight of the ball (Figure 1.16). As the tennis ball makes contact with the tennis court, the ball will behave in a highly predictable manner. A *topspin action* will hit the court surface with a high, deep bounce due to the forward rotation of the ball. A ball hit with *underspin* is usually hit with power and at a low angle, thus creating a skidding action as ball meets surface. The *sidespin* strikes the court with the same action and direction as the sidespin on the ball.

Action of ball striking court — topspin

Action of ball striking court — underspin

Action of ball striking court — sidespin

Figure 1.16   Basic actions for ball striking the court.

In summary, there is a cause-effect relationship to racket control and spin of the ball. A flat racket face at contact will cause a flat flight pattern and flat equal angle bounce off the court. An open racket face will result in underspin during the flight of the ball and a skidding action upon contact with the court surface. A closed racket face will provide a topspin ball action with a resulting high and deep bounce off the court surface. The player should understand that there is only a subtle change in these two racket positions for the slice and topspin groundstrokes at contact.

A closed racket face striking the ball on the side will create a sidespin action followed by a sideward bounce when the ball strikes the court. The beginning player needs to understand the various spins applied to a ball in order to cope with balls hit with spin, and to learn how to supply spin to various strokes.

TYPES OF STROKES

As an introduction to the preliminaries of the strokes in tennis, a definition of the *various strokes* should aid in a more complete understanding of the basic skills of the game.

The basic *forehand groundstroke* (Figure 1.17) is a stroke hit from the baseline following the bounce of the ball. The stroke is executed with a swinging action that produces a flat, no-spin (actually, a small amount of topspin is found in most flat shots) movement to the ball. The *backhand groundstroke* (Figure 1.18) is played under the same conditions as the forehand groundstroke with the same ball action. Both are swinging action strokes with the forehand hit on the

Figure 1.17
Forehand groundstroke.

Figure 1.18
Backhand groundstroke.

racket side of the body and the back-hand hit on the non-racket side of the body. Both strokes are foundations for more advanced strokes, including *top-spin* and *slice (underspin) ground-strokes. Approach shots,* which are an extension of groundstrokes, are characterized by a player advancing to the middle of the court to hit a ball. All *lobs* (Figure 1.19) are also an extension of groundstrokes in terms of the swinging action except there is a lifting action designed to hit the ball deep to the baseline and with a loft.

The *volley* (Figure 1.20) is a punching action characterized by playing the ball prior to contact with the court surface. Both forehand and backhand volleys are usually played at the net, with *half-volleys* being an extension of a volley shot.

The fourth type of stroke is the basic *flat serve* (Figure 1.21), and it is described as a throwing action. Strokes that develop from the flat ser-vice are the slice service (sidespin), the topspin service, and an advanced stroke known as the American twist (another sidespin rotation). The *over-head smash* (Figure 1.22) is a contin-uation of the basic flat service, with the key parts of the serve reflected in the smash. It differs from the serve in that the ball is hit either on the fly or after a bounce on the court surface when the offensive player is posi-tioned near the net.

Figure 1.19 Lob.

Figure 1.20 Volley.

Figure 1.21 Flat Serve.

Figure 1.22 Overhead Smash.

FEEL AND TIMING OF THE TENNIS BALL

The development of a *timing and feel for the tennis ball* is a prerequisite for successful tennis play. Regardless of the racket control, the spin of the ball, and various stroke fundamentals, the execution of each stroke is depen-dent on feeling and timing of the ball through *eye-hand coordination, tim-ing,* and *focus.* Eye-hand coordination is based on past experiences of throwing and catching an object similar to a tennis ball in size. The swinging, throwing, and punching actions associated with tennis are fundamental to the ball games of batting, throwing, and catching that most American chil-dren play during their childhood. If you have played softball or racquetball, or have engaged in activities like playing catch, the game of tennis will

Figure 1.23   Position of ball and feet away and behind the ball.

be easy for you compared to individuals who have not had those experiences.

Timing is also related to where the ball will eventually be positioned to be hit rather than where it bounced originally. You must comprehend where the ball will go after it bounces, and set up behind and away from the ball so that you can step into the ball to hit it (Figure 1.23). Players tend to get too close to the ball or too far away, which causes them to lurch to hit the ball rather than smoothly stepping into the ball. If the ball is too far away, the player can adjust (and not lose timing), by stepping toward the ball with a weight transfer (Figure 1.24). If the ball is too close, the player should step away, yet forward, to hit the ball (Figure 1.25). The key factor in stepping away is the opening of the upper body as the racket is brought through the ball at contact.

Part of timing involves controlling the racket head speed. Players under pressure tend to swing too hard or fast, particularly with the return of service. You must remember to play from a relaxed position and control the racket head speed. The same experience occurs with hitting overhead smashes and groundstrokes when the opposing player is at the net. The added pressure tends to break down timing, forcing the player to rush through the stroke. The focal points have to be relaxation, confidence in hitting the ball, and concentration on the ball. Timing is improved immeasurably by watching the ball as long as possible. This is the part of focus that is most often ignored.

The ability to *focus* is extremely important in tennis. The ability to "see" the ball and perceive the racket striking the ball will help the developing player improve rapidly. Being able to focus on the ball is based on the same past experiences as with eye-hand coordination. The recognition of the bounce of the ball in terms of height, the distance the ball is in relation to the player, and the relationship of the ball to the body are part of the focus concept. Additional focus points include moving to the ball, transferring weight into the ball at contact, and being in the correct position at the correct time. A final consideration is the ability to block all outside distractions and focus on the tennis ball as the only target.

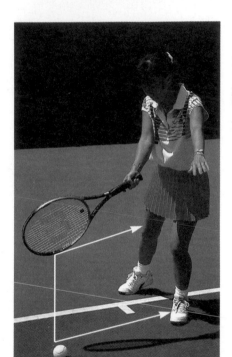

Figure 1.24
Stepping into the ball.

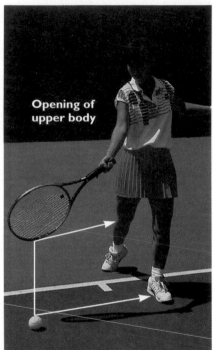

Opening of upper body

Figure 1.25
Stepping away from the ball.

The foundation for timing and feel of the ball rests with establishing a *ready position* from which to hit groundstrokes and volleys (Figure 1.26). The ready position is the first actual skill presented for the developing player, and it is the foundation for all strokes.

The feet should be spaced slightly wider than shoulder width and should be parallel to each other. The knees are slightly bent, and the weight of the body is centered over the balls of the feet. The buttocks should be "down," with the upper body leaning slightly forward in a straight alignment. The head should be "up," looking toward the ball on the opposite side of the net. The racket is held "up" with a forehand grip on the handle, with the non-racket hand lightly touching the throat of the racket. The racket head is above the hands, and the elbows are clear of the body.

The ready position gives the player the opportunity to move equally to the right or left, as well as advance forward or retreat backward. The first response from a player in the ready position is to immediately rotate the shoulders when the direction of the ball from across the net is recognized (Figures 1.27–1.28). A player with good mobility will be able to move the feet quickly from the ready position. If a player can be relaxed in a ready position, keep the weight on the balls of the feet, and then react to the approaching ball with an early turn of the shoulders and quick foot movement, the stroke has been initiated positively.

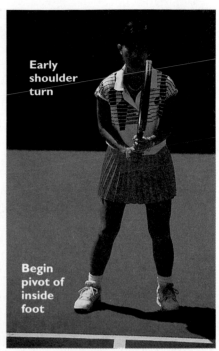

Figure 1.26 Ready position for a groundstroke.

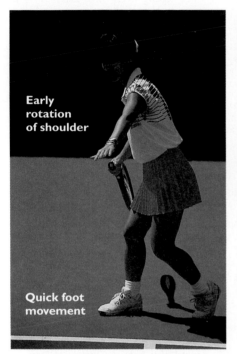

Figure 1.27 Ready position — turn of shoulders (forehand).

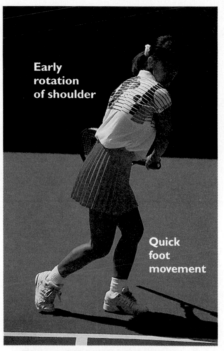

Figure 1.28 Ready position — turn of shoulders (backhand).

LEARNING EXPERIENCE SUGGESTIONS
Ready Position

1. Maintain a base with the feet shoulder width apart.

2. Focus on the ball on the other side of the net.

3. Keep the knees slightly bent and the weight on the balls of the feet.

4. Be relaxed and ready to react.

5. As the ball crosses the net, turn the shoulder and move the feet.

ELIMINATION OF ERRORS (Ready Position)

The Error	What Causes the Error	Correction of the Error
Falling off balance.	Feet too close together.	Widen the base.
Miss-timing the ball.	Not focusing on the ball and not getting shoulders rotated early with feet moving.	Watch the seams of the ball and rotate the shoulders early.